David E. Clarke, Ph.D.

Copyright 2024 David Clarke

ISBN 979-8-218-97524-1

Printed in the United States of America

DAY 1

The Truth from God The narc's Sins are 100% his Fault

The Moment from God After suffering for years in my marriage I sat quietly(which I do not typically do as I enjoy busyness). I asked God to show me clarity in my situation.

I waited a little bit but something truly felt off, so I decided to see if he was just on the way home and much to my surprise he was at a female coworker's house at 10:30 pm. I was blown away.

Of course I called him out on it and the story changed several times on his end. But I know what I saw on my phone that night and even took a picture as a reminder. Facts don't lie. The gaslighting was not going to work any longer. I knew what I would have to do and not to sweep it under the rug as I had with things in the past. There was no more room under the rug.

The next several days were painful after our talk. We had a sit down on a Saturday morning and the lovebombing began. I had so much invested in this marriage and trying to cover for all the stuff. I got blameshifted and was told I better own my 5% of this or he is not going to speak to a counselor or do anything for that matter.

I kept slipping further and further down, then a few weeks into this as I continued to pray for clarity I found out about a secret bank account and 50,000 he had cashed in from stock and paying off another credit card I didn't know

3

I WILL BE FREE

52 God Moment Devotionals on Your Road to Leaving the narc

David E. Clarke, Ph.D.

To all those who send me their freedom stories, and to every person fighting to escape a narc about. That was it. God put it all out for me clearly to see and so big that no rug would cover it.

I am in the process of getting divorced and while I'm certain I'm doing the right thing, the heartbreak of looking back is heavy. My daughter deserves not to see me struggle any longer so I am letting God light the path as only he can. One day at a time, one step at a time. Generational changes must take place and be talked about. I am blessed.

The Word of God Romans 2: 5-6 "But because you are stubborn and refuse to turn from your sin, you are storing up terrible punishment for yourself . . . He will judge everyone according to what they have done."

The Comment from DC (Dave Clarke) The narc always blames you for his sins. He will be shocked when he stands before God and will face the full consequences for his actions. God will not allow him to blame anyone else for what he has done.

The Prayer to God Dear God, help me to get rid of my false guilt for the actions of the narc. Help me to see that I have zero responsibility for the narc's sins.

DAY 2

The Truth from God Face the Evil Done to You

The Moment from God I finally realized the extent of the evil done to me when writing the throw up letters(homework from your book, *I Didn't Want a Divorce, Now What?*). I cried and cried and cried . . . such a great release.

God is so faithful even when it seems He doesn't care about your life or is there with you. He is . . . He's just busy working out His best plans for our life.

My pastor said if I was 100% perfect he would or could still choose to have this affair and leave me. It was his choice . . . I didn't make him do anything!!!!!

Thank you for all your help. It has been a very, very long haul, but by God's grace I am seeing things in a much better way and trusting God's perfect plan for my life.

The Word of God Psalm 41: 9 "Even my best friend, the one I trusted completely, the one who shared my food, has turned against me."

The Comment from DC Your spouse is the one person you were most vulnerable with. The one person you trusted with your heart and your life and your dreams. This person has betrayed you as no one else could.

And the betrayal doesn't have to be adultery, though that certainly qualifies. All the narc's abusive words and actions are also in the betrayal category. All abuse is betrayal.

5

The Prayer to God Dear God, it's so hard to believe that my spouse has intentionally betrayed me and harmed me over and over again. Help me face this awful truth and get away from this evil person.

DAY 3

The Truth from God There is No Truth in the narc

The Moment from God Dear Dr. narc, I have never been so happy to accidentally stumble across a YouTube channel as I have been for yours. I've been married for 24 years (together for 29) and found out 10 months ago that my husband was cheating on me. He gaslit me for months about it.

When shown a picture of him leaving a hotel one morning (after an overnight stay) hand in hand with his girlfriend, he claimed it was photoshopped. There is no truth in this man, and I was devastated to realize that he probably never loved me for the length of our marriage. We have twins who are teenagers. He has lied to them and they don't believe a word he says to them.

After an increase in emotional/verbal abuse 5 months ago, he pushed my daughter & me, and I had him arrested. He managed to get the charges dropped, I'm still not sure how. He is no longer allowed in our home thanks to my attorney making the criminal charge into a civil matter rolled into the divorce proceedings, which is a huge relief.

My kids remark frequently how much more PEACEFUL it is in our home without his bad language and abusive attitude and actions. We are in the middle of the divorce and trying to be civil for the kids' sakes. He frequently calls and texts and wants us ALL to go to dinner together. I try to encourage him to take the kids, but he hardly ever does anything with them outside of attending their events(soccer, dance).

I don't know how much help this will be to others since I'm still in the thick of it, but I can tell you in the last few months, I've noticed myself becoming mentally stronger and I'm rediscovering who I am and what I like and don't like. My time with the kids is relaxed and so precious. There is no pressure to "walk on eggshells" around here anymore. It's such a relief!

The Word of God Psalm 5: 9 "Not a word from their mouth can be trusted; their heart is filled with destruction. Their throat is an open grave; with their tongue they speak deceit."

The Comment from DC The narc lies like he breathes. It is automatic for him. He lies beautifully. He's very persuasive because he believes his own lies. Believe what God says in this passage: you can't trust a word that comes out of the narc's mouth.

The Prayer to God Dear God, I have believed so many of the narc's lies. He has fooled me so many times. I've wanted to believe him, and part of me still does. Please make all of me believe that I can't trust anything he says.

DAY 4

The Truth from God See Yourself Through God's Eyes

The Moment from God After a 20 year marriage, my(now)ex-wife filed for divorce. She had an emotional affair. I hadn't realized that she was a narcissist until I tried to make sense of the paperwork she filed in a failed attempt to get a restraining order against me. As I learned more about narcissism, I saw the truth of who she is and the damage she had inflicted upon me.

Through counseling, incredible friendships, my church, and most of all, God, I can see how much healthier I am in spite of the pain I have gone through over the last few years. I have worked hard to learn to not have to second guess my decisions based on what she would think. I am able to choose things that are good for me and my children without having to care about her view of my choices.

Being able to see myself through God's eyes instead of always feeling that nothing I can do can measure up to her expectations has been so refreshing for me. I still have more work to do on learning to trust people since she really messed me up in being able to trust others. Having friends forgive me with no strings attached is such a blessing that I am not used to experiencing.

In spite of the pain of being divorced, I have a peace that has not been there in years. I am praying that my children can find that peace as well. Unfortunately, they still have to live with her some of the time and deal with her narcissism and lies. I pray that at some point in the future,

God will bless me with a healthy relationship. God is good all of the time.

The Word of God Isaiah 43: 1 "But now, this is what the Lord says-he who created you, O Jacob, he who formed you, O Israel: 'Fear not, for I have redeemed you; I have called you by name; you are mine.' "

The Comment from DC Do you understand how much God values you? This verse shows you how God sees you. He brought you into existence. He made you exactly who you are. He sent Jesus to die for you. He knows you intimately. You belong to Him. You are his precious child and always will be.

The Prayer to God Dear God, help me see myself through Your eyes. The narc has made me believe I am worthless. That is a lie. I am Your priceless, incredibly valuable creation. And because of that, You would never want me to stay with someone who thinks I have no value.

DAY 5

The Truth from God Love Yourself Again

The Moment from God After years of abuse, I filed for divorce. That's when the lovebombing began again. Flowers on the counter before I moved out, when only months before he complained that fresh flowers bothered his allergies while tossing a vase full of a fresh bouquet into the garbage.

When he started facing reality and realized I was not returning, not stopping the divorce, again it was my faith he attacked. How HE was upholding his vows and "YOU pretend you are a Christian but are breaking yours."

My divorce was finalized, and I now try to stay as no contact as sharing custody will allow. He has found new supply and I pray for her. My peace has taken time. I've survived nearly a year divorced now and can say that I'm finally not physically affected by the narc post-abuse symptoms.

I am happy, peaceful in my modest life and I love myself again, for the first time in 16 years! Dr. Clarke, you have helped me and given me strength through this journey by connecting my experience with the support of Scripture and emphasizing what God truly wants for ALL his children in this short time we spend on this earth.

The Word of God John 3:16 "For this is how God loved the world: He gave his one and only Son, so that everyone who believes in him will not perish but have eternal life."

The Comment from DC God loves you more than anyone could ever love you. He sent His only son, Jesus, to die for you. God did that because He wants to have a personal relationship with you.

When you believe Jesus died for your sins-past, present, and future-and rose from the dead, you begin a permanent relationship with God. And God will never, ever stop loving you. He will never, ever leave you.

When you have a relationship with God through Jesus, you will experience what this dear abuse survivor has:

Happiness

Peace

A new life here on earth

The ability to love yourself

Eternal life in Heaven

And when you know God through Jesus, you have His power to fight the escape war and get away from the narc.

You can begin your relationship with God right now by saying the words of the following prayer.

The Prayer to God Dear God, I know I am a sinner. I've made many mistakes and sinned in my life. I realize my sin separates me from You, a holy God.

I believe that Your son, Jesus Christ, died for my sins, was buried, and rose from the dead. I give my life to You now.

The Truth from God The narc Wants to Shame You

The Moment from God I am still married to my narc husband but I left our house and we're in the process of a nasty financial separation. However, God is here by my side every step of the way.

I was sexually abused as a child and my husband knew that. Apart from the childhood abuse, I had kept myself for him. So I still felt like in a way I was still a virgin, at least not physically. When I said to him that I was glad I had kept myself for him and still felt like a virgin he would call me a liar and say I can't be a virgin if I was abused sexually. He didn't understand my perception no matter how much I tried. My psychologist said that the fact that he kept saying that again and again is like he is continuing the childhood abuse that I suffered.

4 years or so ago I had never heard of the term coercive behavior. I reached out to my pastor who talked to me about my husband's behavior with me and explained how this is not biblical and it's coercive.

I knew there was something wrong in his behavior with me but sadly, my husband had convinced me all through these years that I was the problem. I needed to change and it was the only way this marriage was going to work.

The Word of God Isaiah 54: 4 "Do not be afraid; you will not suffer shame. Do not fear disgrace; you will not be humiliated. You will forget the shame of your youth and remember no more the reproach of your widowhood."

The Comment from DC What kind of evil monster shames you for being sexually abused as a child? The narc, that's who. The narc will use whatever he can to keep you in constant shame.

God promises that you will not remain in shame and disgrace and humiliation. As you escape the narc, you will leave all your shame and the traumas attached to it behind.

The Prayer to God Dear God, the narc has worked hard to keep me in shame. I claim this verse and Your promise that I will forget all my shame and all the pain of this abusive marriage.

DAY 7

The Truth from God Jesus Understands Hatred and Persecution

The Moment from God After a 17+ year marriage, I am finally free. Most of the abuse came in the form of sex: unwanted pictures, never showering alone, being awoken at night, never being able to say no or silent treatment until I said yes, etc.,

As a young, people pleasing virgin, now 40 year old who knows she only has to please God, I feel free to share what God has done. The moment I saw all that had happened in those 17 years with a clear lens, I called my mother and said, "I am dirty because of him, and I cannot do this anymore."

I remember the day like it was yesterday. When I told my now ex-husband I wanted a divorce, he called friends and church leadership and told them I was running off with another man. I did not know he said this until just a couple of months ago.

During my marriage, I was compared to pornography and his own extramarital affair. My no's were never no's and my voice was never heard. Rumors were started about me. People turned their backs on me, and I sat in isolation thinking I was hated by all the people I had once trusted.

My children also see with a clear lens, yet they are made to spend 50% of their precious time with him. He stole journals of mine and my oldest daughter. He ripped

15

pages from them. He recorded private conversations of ours. He lied about things my children saw with their own two eyes.

He called the police on me and took me to court after my daughter wanted and needed to be with me "on his day." She came with me with tears rolling down her face, and the beast was released. He got a girlfriend near the end of our divorce, and I continually heard how much better she is than me.

I could go on, but the point I want to make is when God said to me, "my Son who lived a sinless life was mocked, persecuted, beaten, spat upon, ridiculed, lied about, and hung on a cross to die for you, a sinner, saved by His grace. So if Him, why NOT you? Your time in Egypt is almost over!" I remember those words and that moment so clearly which helped me rely so much more on my Savior. He walked sinless all while being persecuted in the worst possible way by sinners.

I should consider it ALL joy while under persecution because the testing of my faith develops endurance. May the storms of life deepen the roots of our faith. The storm is strong, the fight is hard, but with Jesus, we can fight the good fight and finish the race with joy!

When the fight is hard, fight harder with Jesus! I pray my story can encourage others because I have been up against an extreme narcissist who has accused me of being Bipolar and Narcissistic.

The Word of God Hebrews 12: 2-3 "We do this by keeping our eyes on Jesus, the champion who initiates and perfects our faith. Because of the joy awaiting him, he endured the cross, disregarding its shame. Now he is seated in the place of honor beside God's throne. Think of all the hostility he endured from sinful people; then you won't become weary and give up."

The Comment from DC No one suffered on earth like Jesus. He suffered and died for you. He understands the trauma and persecution you are suffering from the narc. He will fight with you as you escape. He will make sure you can endure the pain and break through to joy in your new life.

The Prayer to God Dear God, thank You for sending Jesus to suffer and die for me. I know Jesus gets my pain and is with me as I fight to become free of the narc. Please use my pain to strengthen my faith in You.

DAY 8

The Truth from God You Aren't Crazy and Wicked; the narc is

The Moment from God 12 years of misery, which started literally 2 days after the wedding. I innocently asked him, "so how do you feel being a married man now?" His answer, "I feel like I died and attended my own funeral." He is very well known, liked and highly regarded. But, my covert narc was cruel at home and in private. I spent years living with depression because I felt there was no way out. I felt no one would ever believe me.

I was diagnosed with a rare and inoperable brain tumor. My tumor opened my eyes, and his mask came off. He completely abandoned me, emotionally and physically. He started sleeping in another bedroom. Ignored me, only met my basic needs like driving me to my radiation treatments and doctor appointments because I was on driving restrictions due to seizure precautions.

Suddenly ALL the attention was on me, and my illness. He despised me. I literally felt like he wanted me to die. He never held me, comforted me, zero intimacy, and I later discovered by accident he was on dating sites and had a private Facebook page with only women.

After the discard I confronted him, he denied everything. Said "you're crazy, crazy in the head." Boy that hit hard! One day I was having symptoms in my vaginal area. I immediately went to my gynecologist. Turns out he gave me an STD. I showed him my results, he said, "how do I know I didn't get it from you?"

He ignored the whole issue, pretending like nothing happened. He was fine, whistling, singing every morning like life was just great. Meanwhile I was living in torment, agony, and despair. He didn't want to discuss it, he'd walk away and pretend I wasn't talking, which he so often would do because he knew it would only trigger me.

On my day of freedom, he decided to grab me by my shoulder, turn me around and push me out of the room. I had asked him for a divorce. I reported this to the magistrate the next day, filed a protective order and included the children for various good reasons.

He emptied our bank account, hasn't paid any of our bills, not even our children's private school tuition. He is also facing charges. I bought your books, *Enough is Enough* and *Escaping Your Narcissist*. Read the first, on the second.

The Word of God Romans 1: 29-31 "Their lives became full of every kind of wickedness, sin, greed, hate, envy, murder, quarreling, deception, malicious behavior, and gossip. They are backstabbers, haters of God, insolent, proud, and boastful. They invent new ways of sinning, and they disobey their parents. They refuse to understand, break their promises, are heartless, and have no mercy."

The Comment from DC Does this description in Romans 1 sound familiar? The narc is crazy, but he is much more. He is wicked and sinful in many different ways. He would watch you die and feel nothing. Actually, he would feel happy and relieved. Part of his sinfulness is trying to convince you that you are the crazy, wicked one. Don't buy it!

The Prayer to God Dear God, the narc keeps me confused and feeling guilty. He can convince me that I am crazy, that I am the problem. Help me to see that it is the narc who is crazy, sinful, wicked, and that he is the problem.

DAY 9

The Truth from God There is No Hope for Your Marriage

The Moment from God Oh my! Where to begin? I actively turned to God and prayed to God every day hoping to save my marriage once I discovered my husband was cheating. Only after reading your content have I realized he was/is a narc. I thought that by becoming more holy, more prayerful, closer to God, God would save our marriage. I had hope beyond hope because I had seen the power and felt the presence of God and experienced healings in the past.

I had a couple of dreams . . . in one dream the other woman and he were walking arm in arm very closely together toward me and she said to me, "He's with me now." I saw his '71 Dodge Charger in her garage and her young children's bikes, scooters, toys there in the garage and driveway.

Unfortunately, I didn't "act" upon the messages that were being sent to me. I may have waited way too long(12 years of a 24 year marriage). I really wanted to be a family . . . my husband, my son and me. We both came from broken homes and I really wanted a successful and happy marriage.

I felt I was bending by dealing with his addictions to alcohol, pot, pornography, over-indulging in food . . . but the sin that I couldn't contend with was the long lasting affair with this one woman.

A turning point was when I realized that he didn't respect me and therefore he didn't love me. I knew that I would never go outside the marriage, so I realized that I had to leave the marriage if I want the love from a man in the future.

Before, during, and after the marriage, I've known that I already have the love of God. I cannot imagine navigating this without knowing God. I didn't want to "model" this type of marriage for my son. I wanted to respect myself, so I felt in order to hold myself to the high standard of living and morals that I am entitled to, I needed to leave the marriage.

The Word of God Isaiah 41: 10 "So do not fear, for I am with you; do not be dismayed, for I am your God. I will strengthen you and help you; I will uphold you with my righteous right hand."

The Comment from DC See all the *you* statements in this passage? I am with *you,* I am *your* God, I will strengthen *you*, I will help *you*, I will uphold *you*. This is not about the narc anymore. This is not about the marriage anymore. This is now about you, the hope for your future, and what God will do for you.

The Prayer to God Dear God, give me the ability to let go all hope for my marriage. Enable me to fix my hope on You and the new life You want for me.

DAY 10

The Truth from God God Doesn't Want to Restore Your Marriage

The Moment from God Many years ago, I found myself facing divorce from my so-called Christian husband. I had mentioned that the religious leaders he had followed for several years were not of Christ, and that enraged him. He filed for divorce and I was devastated.

I had been raised with religious expectations of marriage, and one night was sobbing despondently to the Lord and asking Him to restore our marriage. Then I heard as clear as a bell the voice of God talk to me.

He first asked, "do you really want to be married to your husband in the state he is in?" I gave that some quick thought and replied honestly, "well, not really." And then the Lord said, "then stop asking for Me to restore this marriage and consider this divorce My deliverance for you!"

Wow! Short conversation with Jesus that lifted off the depressing burden of trying to figure out how our marriage was going to be fixed! My husband wasn't in agreement with reconciliation, so God was calling me to "come out from among" that marriage so He could be my Father and heal me.

The healing and restoration was truly miraculous and to this day people are shocked when I tell them I've been married before, because not only did the Lord restore me, but He delivered me from any residual spirit of divorce too!

The Word of God Proverbs 3: 5-6 "Trust in the Lord with all your heart; do not depend on your own understanding. Seek his will in all you do, and he will show you which path to take."

The Comment from DC God has no interest in restoring your marriage to the narc. He has a great interest in restoring you. He wants you on the path to divorce, because that is the path of His deliverance for you.

The Prayer to God Dear God, open my eyes and let me see that You want me to get a divorce. Help me see that the divorce is Your deliverance for me.

DAY 11

The Truth from God When It's Time to Go, It's Time to Go

The Moment from God After several months of preparing to leave my abusive husband, I was struggling to figure out how to leave without him knowing so I could avoid his rage. I had been slowly moving extra clothes, papers, and personal items to a supportive friend's home.

I had spoken to a lawyer, my pastor, my Christian counselor, and our adult children so I had a great support system in place. By this time, I had been praying for years that God would change his heart but also mine. I wanted to be a God-centered woman and was seeking both God's Will and for Him to be "in the details."

One evening we had an argument that went on and on. I got ready for bed and was trying to sleep but my husband wouldn't let me rest. He kept trying to argue. Suddenly, a thought entered my mind but it seemed more like the voice of the Holy Spirit. It said, "Time to go."

I got out of bed, packed a bag and loaded my car. In the half hour it took, my husband just sat and watched me from the bed with a snarky, satisfied(and I would say demonic)smile on his face.

I called my friend and told her I was on my way and I never went back. I am at the end of a long and difficult divorce, but God has walked every step with me. Our faithful Lord has truly been "in the details" as I prayed for.

The Word of God Psalm 71: 2 "Save me and rescue me, for you do what is right. Turn your ear to listen to me, and set me free."

The Comment from DC God wants to save you and rescue you from the narc. He hears you, He hears your cries for help. He has a plan to set you free and He will tell you when it's time to leave the narc.

The Prayer to God Dear God, it's hard to know when to leave. Please make it clear to me. When You tell me to leave, give me the courage to leave.

DAY 12

The Truth from God God Chooses You

The Moment from God As I was still in the midst of living with my narcissistic abuser, but had filed for divorce and doing an "in house" separation, I listened to a Christian speaker talking about "asking the Lord what song HE was singing over you?!" I was in such deep need of comfort from Jesus amidst the deep grief I was feeling from my spouse's emotional disconnection, abuse, and rejection.

I sat and prayed to the Lord and asked Him what song He was singing over me. The song He gave me was, "You're Still the One." This brought tears to my broken heart!! I knew the Lord was telling me, "after all these years, I still choose you, you're still the one-I long for relationship with you."

This song from Jesus was so contradictory to what I experienced in a marriage to a man I committed my life to. So thankful Jesus still chooses me and He wants me to choose relationship with Him!

The Word of God Romans 8: 39 "No power in the sky above or in the earth below-indeed, nothing in all creation will ever be able to separate us from the love of God that is revealed in Christ Jesus our Lord."

The Comment from DC You really have no idea just how much God loves you. You are still the one for Him. You will always be the one for Him. If you were the only person on earth, God would love you dearly.

God doesn't care what you have done. He doesn't care about the mistakes you have made. He still chooses you.

The Prayer to God Dear God, sometimes I feel like no one loves me. Like no one chooses me. You are the One I can always rely upon. You will never let me down. Help me to rest in Your great love for me, no matter what happens on my escape journey.

The Truth from God God Will Break Through Your Denial

The Moment from God While I started to recognize abusive patterns in our relationship, I STILL didn't have the courage to leave. But it was obvious the Lord wanted me out.

One night, when my husband was away and had left his old phone at home, I started looking through his old emails, from when we first started dating and got married. And I discovered that he'd been cheating on me from the very beginning. In fact, he never was faithful to me, even in our most "in love" period.

It was like a slap in the face and very painful but it made it crystal clear to me: I CAN leave him. I MUST leave him. No more excuses that he might change or that I was partly at fault for his transgressions. Nope. Discovering the cheating was my ticket out of the marriage because I could no longer find excuses to stay.

In a way, it was the Lord's way of saying: Here you go, now you have a biblical reason to leave! Of course, when I later started to understand the abuse he's put me through other than the adultery, I realized I had had a reason to leave all along. But without that in the face transgression, I don't think I would have had the courage to end it.

The Word of God 1 Corinthians 5: 11 "I meant that you are not to associate with anyone who claims to be a believer yet indulges in sexual sin, or is greedy, or worships idols, or is abusive, or is a drunkard, or cheats people. Don't even eat with such people."

The Comment from DC This passage describes the narc quite well, doesn't it? He calls himself a Christian-check. Sexual sin-probably a check. Greedy-check. Worships idols-check; he worships pleasure and himself. Abusive-absolutely check. Drunkard-maybe check, maybe not. Cheats people-probably check.

This passage says that any one of these narc qualities is reason to cut this person off. "Must not associate" and "with such a man do not even eat" mean not only can you leave him, you must leave him.

The Prayer to God Dear God, thank You for the clarity in this verse. You don't want me anywhere near the abusive narc. Please give me the courage to move past my denial and onto the path of escape.

The Truth from God You've Made the narc an Idol

The Moment from God I began to see that my then-husband had become somewhat of an idol to me. I had lived in fear of displeasing him. He concealed practically all our finances from me. I felt trapped in the marriage even though I am 90% sure he's been involved in extramarital affairs.

I thought staying in the marriage was the obedient thing that I should do as a Christian wife. But I eventually realized that he had taken the place in my life where God was supposed to be.

I recognize that the Lord was correcting me. But even the Lord's correction is liberating. There is grace and love in His correction because He is setting me free to have Jesus in the center of my life. The narc has been "playing God" over me by withholding my own reality from me and manipulating me.

Moreover, we have been misled by the abundance of erroneous teachings within the church that hold us in bondage, in our minds.

And by God's grace, I have been able to "say" to my ex-husband, "get away." (Isaiah 30:22)

The Word of God Isaiah 30: 22 "Then you will destroy all your silver idols and your precious gold images. You will throw them out like filthy rags, saying to them, 'Good riddance!' "

The Comment from DC The narc plays God in your life, controlling you in every area. And you, without realizing it, make him an idol. You allow his control and do all you can to please him.

It's time to get rid of the narc idol, to throw him out of your life like a filthy rag. And in his place you will put the real God.

The Prayer to God Dear God, I confess I have made the narc an idol. I claim Your forgiveness. You are the only One worthy of my worship and allegiance. And You will be the One to get me away from my old idol, the narc.

The Truth from God Do Not Allow the narc to Destroy You

The Moment from God Two years ago, I made the most difficult decision of my life. I put my husband on a plane and sent him away to a center for mental health treatment far away from where we lived. He thought it was for a few weeks. But, I knew that no matter what . . . he was not coming back to live with me. I was done.

I had reached a point where I had to make a decision before I allowed myself to be completely destroyed. The day after he left, I woke and for the first time in years, I was hopeful. I was without stress . . . I was free.

I knew that there was a huge challenge ahead of me but also knew that I had survived things that should have destroyed me and that God had saved me for a purpose.

I was not going to waste this second chance.

The Word of God Deuteronomy 30: 15 "Now listen! Today I am giving you a choice between life and death, between prosperity and disaster."

The Comment from DC You have a choice to make. You can choose life and prosperity by getting away from the narc. Or, you can choose death and disaster by staying with the narc.

It's up to you. God won't force you to make the decision to leave.

God wants you to leave. He wants you to choose life and prosperity. He wants you to be happy and at peace. But, He leaves the choice to you.

Just don't think God wants you to stay and that you are pleasing Him by staying. That's not true. Why would God want you to experience death and disaster? By staying, you grieve God.

The Prayer to God Dear God, up to now I have chosen death and disaster. I thought that I had to stay. I thought that's what You wanted me to do. I want to choose life and prosperity! Please be with me as I make the choice to get ready to leave the narc.

The Truth from God God is Your Husband

The Moment from God Sleep deprivation had become the norm. If he couldn't figure out what my problem was, then no one was sleeping. He had taken to turning on all the lights and standing over me. There was no escape.

One particular night, before he made it to my side of the bed, I had opened up my Bible. I just flipped it open because I couldn't stand to hear the curses he was hurling at me: "I know you want to leave so you can sleep with all the men in town!" "Why are reading that, it doesn't help you!"

I couldn't take it anymore. I cried out in my heart and asked the Lord to show me where He was and to give me hope. It was no coincidence that I opened to Isaiah 54: 5-6.

He said to fear not, I will not be ashamed, my Maker is my husband, I had been forsaken but He promised to gather and redeem me! For every curse thrown at me, God had a promise to replace it with.

That passage got me through that night and many nights just like it, eventually my divorce, and even now I hold it in my heart as a reminder that I was not and never will be alone. Thank you, Lord!

The Word of God Isaiah 54: 5-6 "For your Maker is your husband-the Lord God Almighty is his name-the Holy One of Israel is your Redeemer; he is called the God of all the earth. The Lord will call you back as if you were a wife deserted and distressed in spirit-a wife who married young, only to be rejected, says your God."

The Comment from DC The dirtball narc isn't your husband. He never has been. God is your husband. He will redeem you. He will comfort you, heal your wounds, and love you the way you need to be loved.

The Prayer to God Dear God, this awful man is not my husband. You are my husband. I know I can trust You to treat me with tender care, love, and respect.

DAY 17

The Truth from God Save Your Children From the narc

The Moment from God My breakthrough moment was when my youngest daughter, aged 13, said to me that I must not complain about her pornography use when her dad is cheating on me and also looking at pornography and cheating by looking at other women on his phone.

I have known for a very long time about his porn addiction, but I have just compromised for years already for the sake of our children. My self-esteem is so low, and I have even contemplated ending my life, but I love my children and will never leave them in this world to fight alone.

Through all of this, Jesus has been my guiding light, and He gave me this Scripture in prayer after this incident: Hosea 14: 9.

The Word of God Hosea 14: 9 "Let those who are wise understand these things. Let those with discernment listen carefully. The paths of the Lord are true and right, and righteous people live by walking in them. But in those paths sinners stumble and fall."

The Comment from DC You need to be wise and discerning and understand the truth. And the truth is, by staying with the narc, you do not follow the paths of the Lord. You follow the paths of the narc. Your children will follow his sinful way of life and become like him.

It will take time and great effort, but you can leave the narc. Then you and your children can walk in the paths of the Lord and experience His blessings.

The Prayer to God Dear God, I want to save myself from the narc. But even more than that, I want to save my children from the narc. As I prepare to leave and leave him, I ask that my children will be saved from the narc's influence and that they will walk in Your paths.

DAY 18

The Truth from God Your Home is on Fire

The Moment from God My abuser had moved us from our home state to a very remote area about 900 miles from where we had lived for many years. My friends and family were concerned about me being so far away from my support network.

A friend from home had been reading a book about 9/11 and how the people in the buildings had to make their way down the stairs and out of the buildings . . . she sent me a long email about how I was being abused and how my husband was destroying me and that I needed to climb down the stairs, not ask the fire for permission, and GET OUT of the burning building.

A few weeks later, after pondering on her email and taking it to the Lord many times, I was seriously contemplating leaving with my children to return to my hometown. My husband had hacked into my phone while I was sleeping, found the above email and told me I needed to leave with the kids and go back home. We had sold our home and had nothing there, but I planned to live at my Mother's temporarily.

After a lot of continued confusion about whether to take this massive step, I felt it was still what I needed to do. By Saturday morning, everything was packed. I arose early in the morning and went straight to my closet to pray.

I knelt down and said, "Heavenly Father, if you don't want me to go, I NEED YOU TO STOP ME." At exactly that moment, the smoke alarms in our house turned on full blast and were blaring.

I had to remove them from the walls because they would not turn off. I prayed again and said, "what are you telling me?" He said, "you get your children and get in the car and GO NOW." I did so.

It was only until about an hour later that I made the connection between my friend's email about the burning building and my own "burning building" that the Lord was delivering me from. We made the drive to our hometown and started over with no belongings besides our clothing and toiletries. I filed for divorce for the second time a week later.

Looking back over the following months, the Lord has used this "smoke alarm" experience to remind me repeatedly that I did indeed make the right decision to leave a narcissistic abuser who had no intention of deep change.

His Word is all about deliverance. May you also trust that He wants his daughters to be honored tenderly and respectfully. I am looking forward to a life of peace and self-respect. I have my children, my dignity and the trust of my Father in Heaven.

The Word of God Proverbs 17: 1 "Better a dry crust eaten in peace than a house filled with feasting-and conflict."

The Comment from DC Your home is filled with conflict. Trauma. Unending pain. God wants you to leave so you can experience peace.

The smoke alarms are blaring full blast. Can you hear them now? God is telling you to take your kids and get out.

The Prayer to God Dear God, I am dying in this home. Every day, I die a little more. You are telling me to get out, to save myself and my children. I am going to leave-with You and my children.

DAY 19

The Truth from God Get Away From the Violent narc

The Moment from God After over 20 years of marriage, and escalating abuse(verbal, emotional, financial, and sometimes physical), my narc was removed from the home by police after he became violent and threatening toward me and the children, in a drunken/high state. I was concerned for our safety.

I learned that domestic violence can be throwing things at the person, preventing them from calling 911, and threatening and intimidating them, or breaking things, causing damage. I think more women need to be educated on exactly what domestic violence is, and it can occur even if they don't actually touch you.

I also learned that financial coercive control is another form of abuse (i.e., controlling all of the money, restricting money, hindering someone's ability to work).

After many years and repetitive chaos, I had had enough, and filed for a restraining order against my then husband because he was becoming increasingly dangerous. In the paperwork I filed, I had to write down my reasoning and history of abuse. I documented everything for the court.

I will never forget his initial reaction after first being served with the restraining order paperwork. Instead of apologizing or being upset at the severity of it all, his first words to me were, "I can't believe you put all of this in writing."

42

That was his main concern. Not what he did to me or the kids. Not that he threatened my life. But that I had exposed him by way of written documentation, which was now officially on file with the court. He was devastated that I had revealed what had been going on behind closed doors for years.

It seemed he was not as devastated by what he actually did to us. I am in the divorce and healing process.

The Word of God 2 Timothy 1: 7 "For God has not given us a spirit of fear and timidity, but of power, love, and self-discipline."

The Comment from DC God does not want you to continue living in fear. He does not want you to walk on eggshells and exhaust yourself trying to keep the narc from being violent.

And God absolutely does not want you to be physically abused again by this violent, evil man.

As soon as you can, you need to take your kids and leave this monster. Get to safety and then call the police, get a restraining order, and start the divorce process. Never go back to the violent narc. Never.

The Prayer to God Dear God, I have been living in fear for so long. I never know when the narc will be violent. Please help me to embrace the spirit of power You have already given me. Please protect me and my kids as I plan my exit.

The Truth from God You Will Be Delivered, Healed, and Restored

The Moment from God I had resigned myself to never getting out. Nothing left I could do, but then God said step aside and I will deliver you, heal you, and restore you.

I was driving home from a store. I said nothing, or did anything to warrant the text message I got as I was driving. The narc decided to randomly text me after 35 years of faithful marriage and service that I was no longer being granted wife status. I was no longer serving my only purpose(sex)and I didn't understand what a wife is and does so he was taking my status away.

I broke down that day driving. Ugly crying. I cried out to God in complete despair. The Holy Spirit interceded for me that day.

I asked God, "am I not your daughter? Don't you love me or even care how bad he treats me? I have tried everything to get out and you keep putting up roadblocks. I can't do this on my own. I need your help. Show me you're not ok with this treatment."

God said to me in that moment, "trust me! I will get you out!" 8 months later, I was moved out and filing separation papers, never to return to that evil house.

God reminded me throughout my divorce and all his shady, cheating, underhanded legal maneuvers and all the smear campaign that my Father is in complete control and He would rescue me and take care of my every need.

Divorce is final along with the settlement. I had to medically force retire but my Father is true to His word. All those years and now that I'm free, my health is on the decline, but God continues to protect me from his stalking attempts.

I am healing and growing in His grace. It was my self sufficiency. I will do this. I will do that. Let me make my plans. The moment I broke and turned 100% to my Father and cried out for help, was the moment He started the wheels of rescue. Thank God in all things.

The Word of God Isaiah 43: 2 "When you go through deep waters, I will be with you. When you go through rivers of difficulty, you will not drown. When you walk through the fire of oppression, you will not be burned up; the flames will not consume you."

The Comment from DC You can't avoid the traumas of the escape process. You will go through deep waters. You will go through rivers of difficulty. You will walk through the fire of oppression. At times, you will be certain you won't make it.

But, you will not be destroyed. You will make it. God will be with you every step of the way. God will deliver you, heal you, and restore you.

The Prayer to God Dear God, I know I am not alone in this awful, frightening journey of escape. You are with me. You will protect me and get me through to my new life.

DAY 21

The Truth from God It's Never Too Late to Get Out

The Moment from God When I married my now husband, I'd never met anyone like him before, all the charisma and charm a girl could hope for! Then close to three months in, I started seeing some serious red flags that I unfortunately didn't pay too, too much attention to.

We got married three months into this relationship. BAD move! His true colors of a narc began to pop up everywhere, in every direction!

Jealousy out of control, something I have never dealt with before! In fact, all of this narc behavior I had never even heard about in my life and I was going on 40 years old.

I dealt with this for the first two years into our marriage and it almost drove me out of my mind because I had no idea what I was dealing with. I just knew it was very, very *wrong*.

He moved me away from my three grown children and the rest of my family. But one time when I was visiting one of my kids I ran into a website about narcissistic behavior out of the blue(which I will always believe was my God moment of the start of help).

I have read, and read, and read everything about narcissistic abuse I could find online. Sadly, I've been in this miserable marriage 20 years. I'm working to get out and be free to be me again!

I came across Scriptures as well that convinced me it is not God's will to remain in such an abusive and abandoned relationship.

The Word of God Psalm 146: 7 "He gives justice to the oppressed and food to the hungry. The Lord frees the prisoners."

The Comment from DC Five years. Ten years. Fifteen years. Twenty years. Twenty-five, thirty, forty years. It doesn't matter how long you have been the narc's prisoner. God will give you justice. He will meet your needs. He will set you free.

The Prayer to God Dear God, I am so discouraged and feel hopeless. I've been with the narc for years and it's hard to imagine being free of him. Help me to believe the truth that You want me free and will get me free.

DAY 22

The Truth from God Your Abusive Marriage is Your Isaac

The Moment from God It's not a huge moment, but it's something that hit me while I was reading my Bible study about Abraham's faithfulness to God. In complete faith and obedience, he listened to God, walked his beloved son Isaac up the mountain, built an altar, tied his son and placed him on the altar . . . and of course we know that because Abraham trusted God, that God provided a ram and Abraham's son was saved.

What if the horrible, abusive marriage I've been in for 23 years is my Isaac? What if I have been holding on and desperately trying to look for God to provide a way out of this pain, and refusing to lay it on the altar!????

Maybe I need to finally lay my marriage on the altar of the court system. File the papers and see what God provides. I want to have faith like Abraham!

God can and will provide a ram for me . . . I'm not sure what that will look like. But I know if I have big faith, and let go, he can move in a big way.

I hope this didn't seem silly. It hit me early yesterday morning while I was reading. As I continue stepping out in faith, getting wiser and stronger, I feel God with me. A peace that I didn't have before I was aware of the crazy cycles my narc would keep me trapped in.

I will break free of this toxic relationship and climb the mountain. I will place my marriage on the altar of the courts and wait for God to provide.

The Word of God Genesis 22: 2 "Then God said, 'Take your son, your only son Isaac, whom you love, and go to the region of Moriah. Sacrifice him there as a burnt offering on one of the mountains I will tell you about.' "

The Comment from DC You don't want to give up your marriage. You love the dream of a good marriage. You have worked so hard for so long to save it and improve it.

But God is asking you to give up your marriage. To give it to Him.

Stop hanging onto your marriage. You need to let it go. You need to lay it on the altar and walk away.

Unlike what He did with Abraham, God will not provide a way to save what's on the altar. Your marriage, which is already dead, will go up in flames. That's what it deserves. It's what you deserve because when your marriage burns up on the altar, you will be free.

The Prayer to God Dear God, I don't want to put my marriage on the altar. I don't want to give it up to You. Because I know if I do, my marriage is over. Give me the strength and the courage and the obedience to lay my marriage on the altar and watch it burn up.

The Truth from God You Are Not Alone

The Moment from God My aha moment happened in my 37th year of marriage. My ex, it seemed out of the blue, wanted a divorce and said he was back with his old girlfriend.

I visited a friend for a week and she just let me talk. Everything started to click. "Our" sexual problems weren't all my fault, it was because of the abuse I received from him.

I left and lived with my daughter for 3 months, bought a condo, and filed for divorce. It will be 2 years; our divorce is final in March. I also started the annulment process.

God, my friends, and a great counselor are helping me become whole again. I still have to see him and now his new wife because we have kids and grandkids together. I mostly just say hi and then ignore him if we're at the same event. It's hard but one day at a time.

A song that helps me now is called "A Thousand Years" by Christina Perri. It's my prayer now I put out in the universe for God to send a godly, kind man into my life someday.

The Word of God Proverbs 17: 17 "A friend loves at all times, and a brother is born for adversity."

The Comment from DC When you're in a crisis-and living with the narc certainly qualifies-you find out who your true friends are. Fairweather friends will drop you like a hot rock. They will cut and run. They don't want to get "involved." Never talk to these losers again.

True friends won't just talk, they will act to do whatever it takes to help you get free. They will go through the entire brutal process of escape with you. They'll be with you before, during, and after the divorce.

The Prayer to God Dear God, I cannot go through this nightmare alone. I know I have You and that is most important. But please also provide friends who will support me and help me during and after my escape.

DAY 24

The Truth from God A True Friend Speaks Truth

The Moment from God I accidentally went to a cancelled Bible study at my church. I was in the very center of the church in a darkened room. Being totally alone, this is where I prayed and spiritually was on my knees.

I was there for quite a while, submitting to the Father. I asked God to remove the scales from my eyes, to make clear my path, to point me in the direction of his will and not my own.

It was then that I received a phone call from someone in my church, asking me where I was. I was mere feet away from her. She came to listen, and she had been in a narcissistic relationship years prior, and she pointed out what he was.

Since then, I've been deep diving into the habits & issues with a narc. I was unexpectedly following the advice that Dr. Clarke advised for leaving. I am grateful for his advice, knowledge & encouragement.

The Word of God Proverbs 27: 6 "Wounds from a sincere friend are better than many kisses from an enemy."

The Comment from DC God will bring a true friend to you. A person who understands narcissism and the damage it causes. A person who will not only tell you that you need to leave, but will do all she can do to help you leave.

This person is an angel sent by God to support you, encourage you, cry with you, pray with you, and fight the escape war with you.

It could be a family member. A close friend. A co-worker. A neighbor. A pastor. A pastor's wife. A woman in a Bible study. A Christian counselor. Or, God could bring you a complete stranger.

The Prayer to God Dear God, please bring me at least one true friend. A friend who will speak truth about the narc. A friend who will urge me to leave. A friend who will fight side by side with me as I get away from the narc.

The Truth from God God Will Keep Your Children Safe

The Moment from God As he left the house, I watched him walk down the driveway with my daughter. I knew I had to leave him and the relationship, but I was so scared of what life would look like for my children to be with him alone. I prayed to God and asked him that no matter what happened from this point forward to look after my children and keep them safe.

I then sat down on the couch feeling defeated and alone. I heard a loud tapping noise and looked up to see a bird flapping into the window. This happened about 3 times before he flew away.

I didn't think about it until shortly after and I looked up what that meant spiritually. At this point, I knew it could not have been a coincidence. It was a message from God and he was letting me know we were going to be ok.

In the Bible, birds hold significant symbolism, representing hope, strength, and God's hand in creation and provision.

Consider the role of birds in biblical stories. For instance, Noah used a dove to find land, symbolizing new beginnings and God's mercy. Like the eagle, revered for strength and power, birds symbolize divine protection and guidance. Similarly, the spiritual significance of bird feathers is profound. They often signify heavenly care, reminding us of God's loving presence.

2 months later, I left the relationship. I have a FVRO order in place and my children are with me seeing their father supervised at the moment. I have a long road ahead but I must keep believing that God will continue to guide us and the truth will prevail.

The Word of God Psalm 68: 5 "A father to the fatherless, a defender of widows, is God in his holy dwelling."

The Comment from DC As a mom(or dad), your greatest concern is your children's well-being and safety. It's scary to think about your children being alone with the narc. What should be scarier to you-far scarier-is the damage the narc will do to your children if you stay.

It is only by leaving the narc that you truly protect your children.

The narc is not your children's father. God is. The narc is not your defender. God is.

God wants you to leave and He will keep your children safe from the narc.

The Prayer to God Dear God, I am scared to death to divorce because that means my children will spend time alone with the narc. But I know You will be there with them every second. You will protect them far better than I could.

DAY 26

The Truth from God The narc is Your Enemy

The Moment from God He left 2 years ago at Christmas. We were getting ready to watch a Christmas movie and he disappeared. I found him upstairs viewing porn instead. He then ran away and never returned for good.

He returned on Mother's Day with gifts and his words and touch sickened me. God had removed the fog and I saw the con artist hypocrite that he is and all the past 17 years of lies that I lived. Horrific.

Now I am still dealing with untangling all the years of marriage and a business together. You shared Psalm 141 and 144 as prayers for us and I read them daily. Prayers for war against the enemy.

I am truly grateful for your words of wisdom and encouragement. So many Christian counselors and others do not understand. I know God is faithful and this "war" will eventually end. My son and I will have(and already do)have peace in our home and our hearts.

The Word of God 1 Samuel 17: 45-46 "David said to the Philistine(Goliath), 'You come against me with sword and spear and javelin, but I come against you in the name of the Lord Almighty, the God of the armies of Israel, whom you have defied. This day the Lord will hand you over to me, and I'll strike you down and cut off your head . . .' "

The Comment from DC Goliath was David's enemy and the enemy of his people. The narc is your enemy and the enemy of your children.

Like Goliath, the narc defies God with his sinful, selfish, abusive behavior. The narc is his own god.

The narc is not your husband. The narc is not the father of your children. The narc is not a decent guy who will be reasonable in the divorce process.

The narc is your Goliath. A cold-blooded, arrogant enemy who is determined to ruin your life. He wants to smash you, humiliate you, and take everyone and everything you love from you.

The Prayer to God Dear God, I am not by nature an angry, aggressive person. But I need those traits now in this war with the narc. Help me to see the narc as my enemy, as an evil person who wants to destroy me and my children.

DAY 27

The Truth from God Don't Listen to Church Fools

The Moment from God I want to thank you for your ministry as it has been a huge help in guiding me out of a 35 year demeaning marriage that took from me emotionally, verbally, physically(several autoimmune and gut issues)but not spiritually!

He left the marriage and is pursuing a divorce. I am beyond humbled that God would even supply me with a massive support system, consistent provision and protection and continued encouragement from His word.

After chatting with my pastor, who doesn't know me well and doesn't know my husband at all, but wanted to know my story . . . I mean how do you explain life with a diagnosed(24 years ago)narc!!

The pastor posed some questions that made me doubt and gave the enemy a portal to torment me.

My pastor says it's a pride/sin problem, others say it's a mental health problem. Is it both? One thing I know for sure, it is an evil I have endured from my loved ones(mother, husband, mother in law, and 2 daughters). It is not the Spirit of Christ in them, although 3 out of 5 claim to be Christians.

It is with great humility and praise I stand today better and not bitter after 35 years of torment, mistreatment, and abuse from a man who is tormented himself. May God use this suffering for His glory and the good of all involved. Rejoicing in His mercies that are new each day.

The Word of God Psalm 55: 12-14 "If an enemy were insulting me, I could endure it; if a foe were raising himself against me, I could hide from him. But it is you, a man like myself, my companion, my close friend, with whom I once enjoyed sweet fellowship as we walked with the throng at the house of God."

The Comment from DC Church fools will minimize the narc's abuse, blame you, and try to justify why he acts the way he does. God doesn't care why he is abusive. God cares only about the damage his sin is doing to you.

There is no excuse for the narc's abuse. There is no justification for it.   There is only the need for you to get away from the narc.

Don't listen to anyone-at church or anywhere else-who wants you to stay with the narc. These clueless wonders pretend to care about you. They are fools who couldn't care less about you and your children. Let *them* live with the narc if they want to.

The Prayer to God Dear God, I don't want to please others by staying with the abuser. I want to please You by leaving him. Please bring me persons who understand abuse and want what's best for me and my kids.

DAY 28

The Truth from God God Has Planned Your Escape

The Moment from God This took place over 20 years ago. I was attending a domestic abuse class for victims of domestic abuse at a nearby church. I had been learning about abuse and building up my courage to leave after 20 years of living with a narcissist, suffering emotional abuse and some physical abuse of the children.

My son was now 19 and together we contracted an apartment and were planning to leave the next weekend. God was preparing our escape in a way for us to leave safely.

My son called me from my meeting and said his dad was going crazy because he noticed the money I used from the savings. I got home and saw he was worse than before. I hid upstairs and called the police. They arrived and talked to my husband to calm him down. The kids and I were asked to leave.

My daughter was able to find us a place to stay until our apartment opened up on the weekend. It was amazing how God had planned our safe escape and safe places to stay for 3 nights.

Friends and people from church gave us furniture for our little apartment. Later with police protection I was able to gather some clothes and small items and our 3 pets.

I look back and see now how I had planned my way but God directed our steps(Proverbs 16: 9).

The Word of God Proverbs 16: 9 "We can make our plans, but the Lord determines our steps."

The Comment from DC It's important to make your own plans to escape. My books and video series help you do that. But the great news is, God is completely in charge and already has His own plans to get you out.

Your plans, no matter how carefully you put them together, are flawed. Things will go wrong. Unexpected obstacles will rise up.

No to worry. God has planned your escape and will carry it out!

The Prayer to God Dear God, with Your guidance I will plan my escape. But it is so encouraging to know that You have already planned my exit, to the last detail. I praise You for being a God of faithfulness, organization, and logistics.

DAY 29

The Truth from God Jesus Has Healing Power for You

The Moment from God In my mind, I picture crowds of people reaching out their hand to just touch Jesus. That was all it took to be healed, just the slightest touch.

I picture myself reaching out over someone else, forcing myself through the crowds, wanting to touch Him if only for a second, knowing if it was even just a brush of my hand or one fingertip that He could not even feel, knowing it would change my life forever.

I imagine the people following Him needing to be healed were full of sadness, despair, loneliness, and hopelessness. Others were full of fear, anxiety, and panic. I can see others needing physical healing, the lame, the mute, the blind. I can see the panic in their eyes and on their faces trying to find a way with their physical inability to get to Him.

Those who knew they were powerless. Those who had been abandoned and rejected. I see those who had been abused physically, emotionally, spiritually and sexually. I see people who were never loved, or wanted.

The people who wanted to touch Jesus longed to be healed, to be set free, and be made whole.

Jesus turns and my eyes meet His eyes. I see it in His eyes He loves me and He wants me. Seconds later the very tip of my finger touches the front of His shoulders. His eyes have never left mine.

He whispers you are healed and I love you. I whisper back I don't want You to leave me because I love you too. He assures me He has never left me and never will.

I know for the first time what true love and forgiveness is. My sadness and hopelessness is gone. My feelings of abandonment and rejection have vanished. The void of not feeling loved or wanted is filled with His love and comfort. I found everything I ever needed or wanted in Him.

The Word of God Luke 6: 19 "Everyone tried to touch him, because healing power went out from him, and he healed everyone."

The Comment from DC Only Jesus has healing power. He wants to heal everyone who has been wounded by a narc. He wants to heal you.

As you work on your escape from the narc, Jesus will work on healing you. After you leave the narc, Jesus will heal you as you work through all the traumas. Jesus wants you healed, recovered, and happy.

Do your best to stay close to Jesus by praying and reading the Bible in a daily quiet time with Him, praying throughout the day, and attending a local church where the pastor understands narcissism and abuse.

The Prayer to God Dear God, I know Jesus has healing power and I need healing. I ask that Jesus will heal me from all the wounds the narc and others have inflicted on me.

DAY 30

The Truth from God God Gives You Peace in the Storm

The Moment from God I have been in an abusive marriage for over 15 years now. The abuse started from the very beginning of the marriage. He insults me, invalidates my feelings and concerns, and compares me with everyone possible-his sisters, colleagues, and friend's wives.

Many times I wished I could just disappear from the earth due to the pain and emotional torture.

I have been praying to God for His divine intervention because I didn't have the strength anymore to keep enduring the abuse. One day, a David Clarke video showed up on my thread.

Watching that video was a breakthrough moment for me and my journey to freedom began. I could relate to all that was discussed in that video. That day God told me clearly that I had been released from the toxic marriage(I was always concerned about the 'God hates divorce' clause).

An overwhelming peace came with that revelation and I shed tears of joy and relief. Through that video, I found Dr. Clarke's channel. His videos and stories of survivors are preparing me to leave.

By the grace of God, I have started making plans for a new home and school for my children(two teenagers). We will be leaving this July when my kids vacate from school, though I haven't told them yet so that they don't reveal it to their father before the time is right.

The Word of God Philippians 4: 6-7 "Don't worry about anything; instead, pray about everything. Tell God what you need, and thank him for all he has done. Then you will experience God's peace, which exceeds anything we can understand. His peace will guard your hearts and minds as you live in Christ Jesus."

The Comment from DC You don't have to wait for peace to come after the storm of leaving is over. God wants you to have peace-His peace-*during* the storm of leaving.

The solution to anxiety and worry is continuing to trust in God. Presenting your specific needs to God and thanking Him for His blessings will give you His peace. And that peace, because it protects your emotions and thoughts, will enable you to carry out your plans to leave the narc.

Look, you won't eliminate all anxiety and worry. There will be times when you will freak out, at least temporarily. But, with God's help you can take a big bite out of the fear and anxiety and worry.

The Prayer to God Dear God, I need a lot of things from You in this war of escape. One of them is Your peace. As I pray to You and thank You, please give me your peace so I can do all I have to do to leave.

DAY 31

The Truth from God Leaving is Necessary . . . But Brutally Hard

The Moment from God I've read several of your books. When your book "20 Lies" came out, I heard about and wanted to read it. In the beginning, I hesitated because I knew the "truth" that was in your book.

I put it off for months. Was it God nudging me? I kept hearing about your book, reminders about your book. I took it as a nudge from God to go ahead and purchase the book.

I took an entire Saturday, went to the beach, your book in hand along with my Bible. I cried and prayed all the way there asking for God's direction and His input. I stayed that entire day at the beach and finished your book. You should see my book, I have highlights, scribbles, notes, etc. on 90% of the pages because they all applied to me and my situation. I had my answer.

I still struggle with major guilt. Not sure how to overcome that. But I'm starting to have high days considering even after leaving. It's a constant wave of emotions-ups and downs.

The Word of God Habakkuk 1: 2-3, 5 "How long, O Lord, must I call for help? But you do not listen! 'Violence is everywhere!' I cry, but you do not come to save. Must I forever see these evil deeds? Why must I watch all this misery? Wherever I look, I see destruction and violence . . . The Lord replied, 'Look around at the nations; look and be amazed! For I am doing something in your own day, something you wouldn't believe even if someone told you about it.' "

The Comment from DC I love this woman's honesty. So does God. Leaving the narc is the right thing to do, it is the biblical thing to do. But it is incredibly difficult and painful.

Leaving will be the hardest thing you've ever done in your life.

You will question God. You will cry out to Him. You will wrestle with Him. You will battle feelings of guilt. All completely normal. All part of the process of escape.

God's reply to Habakkuk(and to the people of Judah)is His reply to you and your anguish, your struggles, your questions of Him. God says to you that He is at work and you will be amazed at what He does for you.

The Prayer to God Dear God, please be patient with me as I wrestle with You in this hideous process of escape. I believe You have a plan for me, a good plan, and You will carry it out. And I will be amazed.

DAY 32

The Truth from God Whatever the Cost, Leaving is Worth It

The Moment from God Two people I loved and respected. 1)The florist who delivered me flowers for years, after each time my husband abused me. I never looked at her or spoke to her when she delivered the flowers, as I was always afraid of crying and speaking about the unspeakable.

Then one day, as she delivered my regular flowers, she looked at me and said, "may I ask you something? What has your husband done to you that he sends you so many flowers?" All denial instantly left me as reality finally hit me, and we wept in each other's arms. She was so sorry that she hadn't said something years earlier.

2)A pastor who lived far away, who was gentle, courageous and spiritually wide awake. Had the greatest respect for him. Flew to see him during my divorce from hell. He encouraged me with the words, "I don't advocate divorce, but in your case if you don't divorce him, he will destroy you, then your children."

I did finally divorce him, but he paid lawyers to brutalize me and he took everything. Am still running for my life years later, as he's hired thugs to stalk, harass, intimidate, threaten, poison, defame and slander me, as well as hack all my communication. He also paid the police to publicly humiliate me and subject me to police brutality.

But my greatest loss has been, when all else failed to kill me, he took my three precious children. They've been

68

totally brainwashed and removed from my life, after a lifetime of exceptional closeness. Have not seen their smiling faces, nor heard their beautiful voices for 6 years now.

My unwavering Faith in God, and His steadfast love, presence and protection, have kept me standing. The joy of the Lord is my strength, in a country that has the highest rate of abuse against women in the world. We are a nation of misogynists in every walk of life.

The Word of God Psalm 23: 4 "Even though I walk through the valley of the shadow of death, I will fear no evil, for you are with me; your rod and your staff, they comfort me."

The Comment from DC Getting ready to leave, leaving, and divorcing the narc is walking through the valley of the shadow of death. The narc, who is evil, will make your escape as miserable and traumatic as he possibly can.

As this dear narc survivor found, the cost of escaping is very high. Heartbreakingly high. But, God is with you. He will protect and comfort you.

And you must believe, the cost of staying is far higher. Leaving is always worth it.

The Prayer to God Dear God, leaving the narc will be a nightmare. Living with him is a nightmare. Please calm my fears and give me Your protection and comfort. No matter the cost of escaping, I know You are with me.

DAY 33

The Truth from God God Does the Separating

The Moment from God I was married to my wife for 23 years. I had a weak character, was trauma bonded and codependent. Yet, I was blind to it all and I didn't realize my predicament.

Until by chance, I had a long unrelated conversation with a friend. It was during that conversation that the spell was broken and I realized that I could not properly communicate with my wife and that it would never improve. I didn't understand why at that time, but it was a clear message to me from God.

From that day, my wife sensed that something had changed in me(God had turned off my heart to her)and her torment of me increased.

Later I discovered narcissism through YouTube-Dr. Clarke and others, which was liberating. However, this verse was important to me: Mark 10: 9

The whole concept of divorce caused me angst, and I did not take it lightly, but I realized that God separating what he has joined does not necessarily require the death of one of the parties.

The vows were voided. Though it was a legal marriage, it was actually a form of slavery for me instead, like the Israelites in Egypt.

But God was gracious, and delivered me. I was able to leave after 3 months. God was gracious and I was carried on eagles wings.

The Word of God Mark 10: 9 "Therefore what God has joined together, let man not separate."

The Comment from DC God, not you or your spouse, will separate you from your marriage. God is the only One who has the authority to end a marriage. He will turn your heart off to your narc.

The Prayer to God Dear God, I want the end of this marriage to be Your decision, not mine. To make it clear that divorce is what You want, and to protect me from ongoing pain, please turn my heart off to the narc.

DAY 34

The Truth from God God Has Released You From This Marriage

The Moment from God Very short version of a 36 year narc marriage. After 2 attempts of going back into an abusive marriage, the third time God released me and this is how.

After a bad day working with my spouse in a business we owned, I decided to go home early. I mowed the yard, afterwards showered. I was at my wit's end. I had prayed for years to try and make this marriage work and I was desperate.

My prayer went something like this: "God, I can't do this anymore. I am tired and I feel like I am dying. Please show me, tell me and be so obvious it's coming from you because I can't do this anymore."

Sobbing the whole time. Grieving because I felt like such a failure. I got up from the floor.

Spouse came home and called me down from upstairs and told me to GET OUT and I had until Sunday. This was Friday. I asked him are you sure and he said, "Don't let the door hit you on the butt on the way out."

I confirmed to him I would not ever come back and he said he didn't care. I felt such a relief! God just released me from a 36 year struggle. I knew this was my chance to have a new life. It has been hard but peaceful.

The Word of God 2 Timothy 3: 1-5 "But mark this: There will be terrible times in the last days. People will be lovers of themselves, lovers of money, boastful, proud, abusive,

72

disobedient to their parents, ungrateful, unholy, without love, unforgiving, slanderous, without self-control, brutal, not lovers of the good, treacherous, rash, conceited, lovers of pleasure rather than lovers of God-having a form of godliness but denying its power. Have nothing to do with them."

The Comment from DC Have you ever read a better description of a narc than the one in 2 Timothy 3: 1-5? I haven't. God not only describes a narc, He bluntly tells you to leave the narc.

Not, you can leave if you want to. Not, it's okay to stay. God, through Paul, says *leave the narc*.

There are no exceptions in this passage. It doesn't say at the end, "unless you're married to a person like this." It says, "have nothing to do with them."

You don't have to wait 36 years like the dear soul in today's devotional. Praise God she is free now. Your release from God can be right now. No matter how many years you've been with the narc, God has released you and you can start your journey of escape.

The Prayer to God Dear God, thank You for releasing me from my marriage. I know You do not want me to stay with this monster. Thank You for loving me and not wanting me to continue suffering with the narc.

DAY 35

The Truth from God You Can Biblically Divorce the narc

The Moment from God I was unable to figure out my husband's years of yelling, verbal abuse, control, and making me his scapegoat for his actions, until now! After almost 41 years I get it! I was married to a narc(who was raised by a narc).

It will be 3 years in May since I left him. It has not been easy. I was 61, had to find a job(hard at my age), and a place to live. I am so much healthier and so happy to not be dealing with the stress he brought on me.

Through God's goodness and grace, my adult children have turned out well, and serving the Lord. I have filed for divorce. He is doing his best to keep the divorce from going forward, but I will not stop until it's done.

I also want to say that as a Christian, I knew full well what the Bible says about divorce, and the shame and fear of filing for a divorce was hard. Keep telling women that in their situation God is for them and is not okay with the narc's behavior. What a relief!

FYI, Chuck Swindoll did a sermon on divorce. He had once believed divorce was wrong but has totally changed his mind.

The Word of God 1 Corinthians 7: 15 "But if the unbeliever leaves, let him do so. A believing man or woman is not bound in such circumstances; God has called us to live in peace."

The Comment from DC In this passage, Paul teaches that chronic abuse-physical or emotional-is a biblical reason for divorce. "In such circumstances" refers to other painful relationship conditions, not just abandonment. One of these circumstances is abuse.

Paul is saying-God through Paul-that abandonment by a nonChristian spouse and other similarly destructive circumstances-such as abuse-are grounds for divorce.

God wants you to divorce the narc because He wants you to stop being traumatized. God wants you to "live in peace."

The Prayer to God Dear God, thank You for not wanting me to continue to suffer in this marriage to the narc. Thank You for providing a biblical reason to divorce this awful, abusive narc.

DAY 36

The Truth from God Choose Life by Choosing Divorce

The Moment from God After a marriage of 2.5 years, I reached the conclusion that this was a hopeless situation. It took a counselor, my sister, podcasts(such as yours)to educate me what a **narcissist** is and the understanding that he was not going to change.

Although a divorce was the last thing I wanted, I realized there was no other choice. What I have **gained** was **worth the pain**. What I had to go through to get to this place, I now have freedom.

I am no longer living with someone that is a fake, fraud, liar, immature, irresponsible and only concerned about impressing others. Living with a narc is destructive and toxic.

From the beginning, he disrespected me, ignored my boundaries, disrespected me in every way! He began tracking me(my phone, car, etc)for no reason. This narc was controlling, manipulating and nearly cost me my life and my job.

Fortunately, I had wise counsel that affirmed divorce was my only option. I was willing and went for counseling for myself as he was adamantly opposed to it and now two years later, my health is restored as well as my finances. I am creating a meaningful, God-centered life and I have peace, joy and my life back.

I would say to anyone that is in a situation like I was, listen to people like Dr. Clarke because everything he has said

76

I have experienced myself. I have no regrets. I am only sorry that I didn't know what kind of person he was before I married him. Don't wait!

The Word of God Deuteronomy 30: 19-20 ". . . Now choose life, so that you and your children may live and that you may love the Lord your God, listen to his voice, and hold fast to him. For the Lord is your life . . . "

The Comment from DC When you live with a narc, you really have no choice but to divorce him. He will not change. He will continue to damage and traumatize and destroy you and your children.

God wants you to choose life. Since there is no life with a narc, that means you need to choose divorce. After your escape, you and your children can truly live in a close relationship with God and with each other.

The Prayer to God Dear God, I know You want me to choose life. Help me see that while divorce is the death of the marriage, it is the beginning of life for me and my children.

DAY 37

The Truth from God Christ Gives You Strength

The Moment from God Our marriage took place only because of trauma, specifically because I married him 2 weeks after I found out I was pregnant. And the only reason I was pregnant was because he sexually violated/raped me 2 months prior.

When I had to marry him I knew that I could only do it because I knew that "I can do all things through Christ who gives me strength" and I did it.

This has been the cry of my heart the entire duration of our(almost)29 years of a very destructive marriage. This continues to still be the same cry of my heart to God knowing how desperately I need to get out, and as I am approaching the necessary exit of this destructive marriage. And also will continue to be as I navigate life on the other side of this marriage.

Yesterday, today and forever: "I can do all things through Christ who gives strength."

The Word of God Philippians 4: 13 "For I can do everything through Christ, who gives me strength."

The Comment from DC This sweet lady has endured awful trauma by the narc from early on in their relationship. So have every one of you reading this.

You have spent years relying on Christ to give you the strength to endure the abuse, survive, and stay. Now, it's time to rely on Christ to give you the strength to leave the narc.

You don't have the power to leave. In your own strength, it's impossible. You're not getting out. But, Jesus has all the power in the Universe and He will give it to you in your escape journey.

The Prayer to God Dear God, I can't get out of this abusive relationship on my own. I claim Your power to get me free of this narc.

DAY 38

The Truth from God Don't Go Back to Egypt

The Moment from God Within one year, I had lost the respect of my children, discovered he had made sexual advances to a few of my friends and began to exploit me financially. He promised me over and over these things were not true and we were a family. That he loved us.

Just as I was about to execute my plan from your book, "Enough is Enough," I got news that my narc had been hospitalized with a critical diagnosis. My pastor and my narc's mother had spoken to him and had faith he had changed.

I let my guard down and allowed him to come back home. I threw myself back into the marriage 100% and cared for him through his illness. (Although my soul never felt at peace)

I prayed very hard one day on my way to the gym that God would reveal to me the truth. I felt in my soul something was still not right. At church the next morning the minister preached on faith. How when the Israelites entered the Red Sea they escaped by faith. They didn't worry about the "how", they were just obedient to God.

One night, I was getting ready to settle in for the night when I received a strange message on LinkedIn. A woman reached out to say she has been my husband's mistress of three years.

After a frightening confrontation with my narc, I made the instant decision to load my precious daughters up in our vehicle, taking only a few suitcases and abandoning everything, to enter the Red Sea and escape my Egypt.

I have been restored to my older sons who lost respect for me when I chose to marry this man. I am surrounded by friends and family. I am still seeking a new church home.

Within three days of returning home, I was able to move into a gorgeous apartment, found a second job, and was blessed with so many unexpected furnishings for my home.

God paved a way for us! I listen to Dr. Clarke daily and enjoy the humor behind his podcasts and videos.

After I left, my spouse and his mistress discovered that they weren't meant to be after all . . . (big surprise) My spouse has asked me to restore the marriage. I truly was tempted to try again.

I confided to my best friend my struggles with the situation. She not knowing about the sermon at church said to me, "Don't go back to Egypt."

Thank you God for your grace and deliverance.

The Word of God Exodus 14: 30 "That is how the Lord rescued Israel from the hand of the Egyptians that day. And the Israelites saw the bodies of the Egyptians washed up on the seashore."

The Comment from DC When God rescues you from the narc and you are away from him, keep moving forward. Don't look back.

Going back to the narc is a horrendous mistake that will cost you dearly. It is also an insult to God, who helped you escape this vile creature.

If you're thinking about going back, don't. If you have gone back, get ready to leave again asap.

Don't go back to your Egypt.

The Prayer to God Dear God, my time in Egypt with the narc was awful and traumatic. I praise You for rescuing me, for parting the sea so I could get out. Give me the courage and faith to never go back.

DAY 39

The Truth from God Don't Return to Your Vomit

The Moment from God My husband and I have been married for over 40 years. Many of those years have been years of emotional, financial and a few times(years back)some physical.

I had separated 2xs before, with my daughters, each time coming back thinking there was a change. It lasted briefly and I was again struggling with his bitter and emotional abuse.

Recently(right before I left for the third time), he added on hours of conversations on the phone with a mutual female friend of ours who was recently divorced. Neither would stop their relationship even after I spoke to them about it.

This relationship with her over the phone emboldened him I feel, to tell me many times, "We need a divorce." "You need to leave." He made life so difficult. However, I was gonna stay and fight it out. My kids were adults so it was just me, I'll handle it.

I felt guilty for not wanting to be around him. Ashamed I had allowed this to happen again. I had to stay, for God and our family. Then my adult children approached me so concerned that this with their dad and I would escalate to something worse, asked me to please leave. My son provided a home for me.

I am out, safe, healing and enjoying life. I have my children, grandchildren and true friends! Thank you Lord for rescuing me even in my ignorance!

The Word of God Proverbs 26: 11 "As a dog returns to its vomit, so a fool repeats his folly."

The Comment from DC This is a graphic, disgusting picture but it is an accurate description of going back to the narc. Going back to a person who has done so much damage to you and your children is exactly like going back to a pile of your own vomit.

We all are fools at times. We all do foolish things we later regret. I could tell you many stories of my foolishness. So, I'm not throwing stones. I am telling you, on the authority of Scripture, do not return to your vomit/your narc.

The Prayer to God Dear God, I am so tempted to go back to the narc. I want to believe he will be different this time. Every time I think about returning, please give me this picture of a dog returning to its vomit.

The Truth from God God Will Do Miracles for You

The Moment from God I have some miracle moments to share. After the last insane incident with the narc when he verbally abused me & told me that I deserved it, pushing me to the point of weeping and begging for him to stop, he showed me that he had been recording me crying and threatened to post it on social media. (he had recorded me crying previously)

That was the breaking point when I felt the scales finally fall off of my eyes. I had been praying to God to show me what was going on. I understood at that moment that the narc was causing me this pain & recording it with the intent to sexually gratify himself to the video later. His causing me pain gave him a sense of power over me.

I moved out with no place to go, but I would have become homeless rather than stay with that demon. My son and daughter in law took me in and gave me a paid job as caregiver for my grandson. That was the absolute perfect situation for me, straight from God's plan.

Of course I couldn't stay there forever, so I put my name on a list for a senior apartment. I was #11 on the list when I called one day recently to check, and they told me that it would be another 3 months before I could get in.

I had been praying about this, when an hour later, the apartment called and offered me an apartment! I move into my place of safety and freedom this month.

Everything has fallen into place so beautifully for me. Thanks be to God. The rollercoaster ride with an evil narc who was a psychotic, adulterous, dishonest liar and gaslighting manipulator is over. It has been 28 years.

The Word of God Ephesians 3: 20 "Now to him who is able to do immeasurably more than all we ask or imagine, according to his power that is at work within us . . . "

The Comment from DC Many of my phone advice clients tell me, "Dave, I need a miracle." I give the same response every time: "God is still in the miracle business. He will do a miracle for you. In fact, He'll do more than one miracle."

As our verse says, God will do much, much more than you can ask. God will do much, much more than you can even imagine.

All along your journey of escape, God will do miracles. The narc will get no miracles. You will get miracles.

The Prayer to God Dear God, I need miracles from You. I believe You will do things for me that I haven't even asked for. Miracles that I can't even imagine.

DAY 41

The Truth from God The Divorce is an All Out War

The Moment from God Was married 10 years to a narc and compulsive gambler/alcoholic. Got a protective order, police removed him from the home. He filed for appeal which judge denied.

Abuses the kids mentally and emotionally, doesn't care about them. Chokes the dogs in the air in front of them. He violated PO. Went to court 12 times. Final court date coming up. Lawyer says it is such a huge case that one court day will not be enough.

He exposed kids to porn and sings sexually explicit songs in front of them, non radio version. Had to get kids a best of interest attorney and they refuse to go with him and I refuse to send them. He filed on me contempt of court 2 weeks ago.

2 homes are mine, I paid with my money, he is trying to get all the money from me. Used me from the start for my money, I see that now. I go no contact with him since the PO, only talk about the kids. We had spent 9 hours in mediation for him to say never mind, I don't agree to any of this.

Praying I come out of this not owing him a penny. He sold his truck I paid for and sold a boat and another car. ALL marital property-I didn't see a penny. He doesn't pay his child support.

The Word of God Psalm 144: 1 "Praise be to the Lord, my Rock, who trains my hands for war, my fingers for battle."

The Comment from DC Divorcing the narc will be a vicious, no holds barred, street to street war. The Moment from God story in today's devotional is not unusual. Like this wretched narc, your narc will do all he can to use and manipulate the legal system and destroy you.

You need to get ready for war. You will be fighting to protect yourself and your children from a heartless, evil scumball. Get my book, *Escaping Your Narcissist*-it will show you exactly how to fight the divorce war.

The Prayer to God Dear God, like David in Psalm 144, I need You to teach me how to fight this divorce war. Make me righteously angry and keep me strong as I fight the narc. Fight for me and beat the narc!

The Truth from God satan(small s) Attacks You Through the narc

The Moment from God During my two years with the narc, I slowly began to get sick. I had many doctor visits in the past two years for things going wrong with my body. I felt like I was dying slowly, not knowing what was happening. I was depressed and oppressed and thought of wanting God to take me home.

My soon to be ex husband is a narc through and through. He uses my healed past against me and calls me nuts to my family, and it's all in love, he says. So clever and sly. Shy and quiet, yet funny and charming. A master divider of family and friends, nothing is sacred.

Since I went to NO contact in early March, my body has been recovering, my energy is returning, and my sleep at night is improving. My anxiety levels are dropping. I notice I am not struggling to breathe and can catch my breath more effortlessly.

The narc continues to contact me through USPS with letters, cards, and emails, blatantly bulldozing down my boundaries. It doesn't matter what you want or need; they only care about what they want.

What took me a while to get was not to open any mail. It is like letting satan out to tear me apart. It's imperative to keep your curiosity in check and don't open anything. Reading his letters of twisted love-hate, condemning comments cost me a lot. I would suffer physically and mentally for it for a few days.

I discovered this isn't some little game that normal couples struggle with. This is a matter of life and death; the demons Jezebel and Leviathan behind the narc will kill you if you let them. Close every door, window and crack into your life. That is how serious this is.

The Word of God Ephesians 6: 11-12 "Put on the full armor of God so that you can take your stand against the devil's schemes. For our struggle is not against flesh and blood, but against the rulers, against the authorities, against the powers of this dark world and against the spiritual forces of evil in the heavenly realms."

The Comment from DC The narc is doing the devil's work against you. You are not only struggling with the narc. You are struggling with satan and his evil schemes.

This is one more reason-the main reason, in fact-that the narc will never change. He is the tool of satan. Though he's too arrogant and blinded to realize it, he is under satan's power and control.

Because you have these two vicious, relentless enemies, you must not show the narc any mercy, any compassion, or any grace in this war to escape.

The Prayer to God Dear God, I am battling two enemies: the narc and his master, satan. Help me to put on Your full armor so You can protect me from their attacks.

The Truth from God Call Me Abba

The Moment from God This moment was pivotal in my relationship with God, and in gaining the strength to face my abusive spouse. I hope it speaks to the heart of another precious woman who needs it.

I was lying face-down on the carpet, crying to God from the bottom of my heart. I was completely shattered, and I could not imagine ever getting up off the floor. "Who are You?!" I yelled at God. "Where are You?!"

I gradually sat up to lean on my bed. I didn't even bother blowing my nose. One moment, I felt alone. In the next, like warm butter, His Presence was next to me. Not above me, hovering, disappointed in me. But pressed to my right side, there on the floor.

Call Me Abba, came the clear, distinct Voice. I knew, more confidently than I had ever known anything, that He was sitting with me, with His arm about my shoulders. "Ok . . . Abba," I said. From that day forward, I knew what I meant to Him.

Several months later, I was waiting outside a pastor's office. It was probably going to be a terrible appointment with my husband and me, and I was scared. I took lots of deep breaths.

In my hand, I held a copy of a book I was returning, and I flipped open to a random page. My eyes fell on a paragraph from Romans 8: "He *causes* us to call Him Abba, Father." I was taken back to that moment on the carpet and to the oh-so-near Presence of my Abba.

He had drawn near to me-little, broken me-and caused me to call him Abba. Daddy. My Protector and Comforter. I strode into the office, sat next to my husband, and enforced my boundaries like a warrior. It was a new day.

The Word of God Romans 8: 15 "For you did not receive a spirit that makes you a slave again to fear, but you have received the Spirit of sonship. And by him we cry, 'Abba, Father.' "

The Comment from DC You are done being constantly fearful of the narc. You have no connection to the narc. You are not related to him in any way. You are the precious child of Almighty God. God loves you, cherishes you, and protects you. You will *always* be His child.

The Prayer to God Dear God, I am so grateful that I can call You, "Abba, Father." As I sever my relationship with the narc, help me grow closer and closer to You, my loving Father.

DAY 44

The Truth from God The narc Will Turn Many Against You

The Moment from God Leaving the narc was the best decision I could have made. I am in the middle of divorcing him still(it's been 5 years)with no end in sight because he is dragging it out.

He turned my church against me, our "friends" against me, our children against me, even my own family of origin colludes with him against me. I have basically lost everything, but in that I found an intimate relationship with God and myself and learned that God is all I need. He has helped purge all the toxic people out of my life.

I was dissociated for the first 3.5 years from all of the trauma, but now I feel joy and peace and have hope for my future-I feel alive again.

I realize that I am getting further and further away day by day from someone who was always working against me, someone who was going to destroy my life. He is losing his power over me and I am gaining my power back. I have learned my value and how to love myself.

I am the lighthouse for my children and the breaker of a generational curse that has plagued my family. It's not easy to be the first one out of an abusive system but I can see it is already changing the trajectory for my daughter and saving her from narcs(which makes it worth it). And it is of course changing my trajectory as well.

I am getting healthier in every way. I am getting stronger. I find myself healthier than most people that have not been forced to do self-work/recovery work. I love my new life, one that is no longer being stolen from me by narcs and it's just beginning.

This has been the fight of my life, and the fight for my life and I am emerging on the other side a better person, the person I have always been inside-like a diamond or a pearl forged from the pressure, or pure gold refined by fire.

The Word of God 2 Corinthians 5: 17 "This means that anyone who belongs to Christ has become a new person. The old life is gone; a new life has begun!"

The Comment from DC When you become a follower of Jesus Christ, you become a new person. You escape your old life of sin and begin a new life.

In the same way, when you escape the narc you become a new person. You leave the narc-and all who believe his lies about you-behind as you begin your new life.

Dump all those betrayers who side with the narc. Go no contact. Just like the narc, they cannot be trusted ever again. They are part of your old life.

In your new life, you will find persons you can trust. Who love you. Who support you completely. Who will walk with you through whatever you face in life.

The Prayer to God Dear God, it hurts deeply to see the narc turn so many persons-persons I thought I could trust-against me. I feel alone and vulnerable. Bind up my wounds and lead me to a whole new group of people who will always love me and have my back.

DAY 45

The Truth from God You Have to Fight for Freedom

The Moment from God My friend shared with me about Dr. Clarke. Wow! A man gets it? I bought his book, Enough is Enough. The validation was life changing.

Then my ex was inappropriate with our daughters. They were in danger. I kicked him out, exposed him to the church(only to have the church turn their back on me).

I suggested to my ex he read Dr. Clarke's book, *I Destroyed My Marriage*. He followed through word for word in the letters, literally. But no behavior changes.

Once I paid off our debt in 6 months, the financial sabotage began. I had had enough and filed for legal separation. He answered with divorce. Then he fought for custody of our minor daughter, but he gets no parenting time with her. She is safe and free.

Trauma bond is real and I broke it. Fear is real and I overcame it. I believed the lies no more. I fought for freedom. I fought for me and my girls.

It was the hardest thing I've ever done. I'm still unraveling the lies. I have changed the generational abuse that has occurred in the last 3 generations of my family. No more.

2 years ago when this process began, I worked part time. Over that period I have been able to adjust to working full time. I am happy. I love me now. I love and enjoy life. I

meet with friends and my communities of support and they help me and my girls grow.

I LOVE the empty space next to me in my bed. I LOVE setting goals and not having someone sabotage them. Since the divorce, the demon I fought with everyday in my head is now gone.

I took my name back and feel empowered everytime I say it. After 27 years, I am free. God fought this battle for me. My job was to heal while he fought for me.

I was terrified in the beginning. He came through. He kept every promise He has ever made. I'm seeing Him restore all that the locusts have destroyed.

The Word of God Psalm 57: 4, 58: 6 "I am in the midst of lions; I lie among ravenous beasts-men whose teeth are spears and arrows, whose tongues are sharp swords. Break the teeth in their mouths, O God; tear out, O Lord, the fangs of the lions!"

The Comment from DC Even though the narc hates you and treats you like garbage, he doesn't want you to leave him. Your departure will make him look bad, cost him his precious control over you, and cost him money.

The narc will fight you tooth and nail for every bloody inch of your freedom journey. He and his evil army of lions will throw everything they have at you and your godly army of supporters.

The narc doesn't realize you have one person in your army who will lead you to victory. That person is God.

The Prayer to God Dear God, I am in the battle of my life. I ask You to deal with the narc and his army. Cripple them, break their teeth, tear out their fangs so I can win my freedom.

DAY 46

The Truth from God Pray for Vengeance

The Moment from God Hi David, my lightbulb moment was your comment to me that made me realize that the only thing benefitting from my panic attacks were the emergency room doctors wallets.

My husband is lying through his teeth about being disabled while he works under the table. I have to continue to pay for everything for him and the kids until our divorce is final which can be a long time.

He is going to get half my retirement after he blew through his retirement on real estate speculation and stick me with 100% of our daughter's student loans if he gets his way and he is an expert at lying.

My question is how do I pray for justice for me and my children, and protection over my finances without praying for vengeance against him.

My only goal is to come out the other side of divorce without bitterness and be able to forgive him, but that's very hard when he is coming after everything of mine while cheating the system.

I know forgiveness is for me and I have to forgive. I am having a hard time getting those words out of my mouth when I really want God to give me justice and expose him, but I don't necessarily want misfortune to come to him.

The Word of God Psalm 69: 24-25 "Pour out your wrath on them; let your fierce anger overtake them. May their place be deserted; let there be no one to dwell in their tents."

The Comment from DC Today's devotional passage is rough, isn't it? David prays for God to treat his enemies with extreme harshness.

David prays for God's vengeance against those who are persecuting His people. David asks for vengeance against his enemies, not just in this passage but in many of his Psalms.

So, pray as David did against your enemy, the narc. This is a war so it is perfectly fine-and biblical-to pray that God will: pour out His wrath on the narc, overwhelm the narc with His fierce anger, and kill the narc.

That's right, kill the narc. When David prays that his enemy's residence be deserted, it is deserted because the enemy died.

And don't spend any time on forgiveness until after the war is over. After your escape and the divorce is final.

This is a time for righteous anger, not forgiveness.

Vengeance is God's business. He'll do it in His time and in His way. But He will do it. Your job is to pray for it.

The Prayer to God Dear God, it feels wrong and uncomfortable to pray for Your vengeance against the narc. But if David prays for it, I guess I can, too. I ask You to deal with the narc harshly, to defeat him, to pour out Your wrath on him. And yes, if it's Your will, to take him out.

DAY 47

The Truth from God Jesus Will Lift Your Burdens

The Moment from God After I found out about my husband's affair, I started packing his belongings into garbage bags and throwing them in the garage. I told him to get out, but knew he couldn't leave for a few weeks.

The first morning after he moved out, a peace flooded over me. God showed me an image of Him taking a huge boulder off of my shoulders and dropping it onto my soon to be ex-husband's shoulders. The weight was lifted by God.

At that moment, I knew He was still in control and I had done the right thing. God is always with me in the good times and bad. He brought me through the hardest time of my life. Glory to Him.

The Word of God Matthew 11: 28-30 "Then Jesus said, 'Come to me, all of you who are weary and carry heavy burdens, and I will give you rest. Take my yoke upon you. Let me teach you, because I am humble and gentle at heart, and you will find rest for your souls. For my yoke is easy to bear, and the burden I give you is light.' "

The Comment from DC Because of all the narc's abuse, you are carrying heavy burdens. You desperately need rest. Jesus sees you and will help you. He will lift your burdens and give your soul rest. All He asks is that you place yourself under His authority and follow His teachings.

The Prayer to God Dear God, You know how weary and beaten down I am. I ask now for the rest Jesus offers me. I ask that You lift my burdens off my shoulders and put them on the shoulders of the narc. As I stay close to Jesus, I know I will endure this awful trial and be at rest.

The Truth from God God is With You After the Divorce

The Moment from God After over 40 years of marriage to a narc, he divorced me when I started to stand up to him. When I began creating a life of my own, it was very difficult because the narc had controlled all finances and most decisions. My father had been this way also.

So the first few years of my life as a single woman were overwhelming and often frightening. One day when I was reading my Bible, I came across these verses that were like pure gold. They have continued to comfort me and give me strength.

That was almost 4 years ago now. My children have turned against me because he was found guilty of contempt of court for refusing to pay me court ordered spousal support. I'm heartbroken and lonely, but remain confident that God will continue to take care of me.

The Word of God Psalm 91: 14-16 "Because he loves me, says the Lord, I will rescue him; I will protect him, for he acknowledges my name. He will call upon me, and I will answer him; I will be with him in trouble, I will deliver him and honor him. With long life will I satisfy him and show him my salvation."

The Comment from DC What a lineup of awesome promises from God! God will rescue you, protect you, answer your prayers, be with you in trouble(and with a narc, there's a lot of trouble), deliver you, honor you, give you long life, and give you eternal life.

Would you like anything else?

God will do all these things for you as you prepare to escape the narc, during the divorce, after the divorce, and for the rest of your life.

The Prayer to God Dear God, it's been incredibly hard and painful living with the narc up to now. I know it will be incredibly hard and painful to prepare to leave, to leave, to divorce him, and to adjust to life after the divorce. But I also know You will be with me, doing all these things in Psalm 91 for me.

The Truth from God God is Your Only Umbrella

The Moment from God As I sat here thinking of all the ways God has shown up for me the past couple years, I keep smiling bigger and bigger. I am bursting with God's goodness and I want other women to hear!

The poisonous teaching that I was steeped in went something like this: God had put me under my husband's protection, and if I stepped out from under it by disagreeing or disrespecting him, I would be exposed, unprotected from satan's fiery darts.

Until one day, a wise woman pointed out how very unbiblical this idea is. How can we *ever* be out from under the biggest umbrella-God Himself? I cherished this new image of my Abba Father being my *only* umbrella.

The next day, I opened my phone and the first image I saw was a book cover. It showed a woman under a strong, red umbrella. I smiled and began to get dressed. Pulling on a new jacket I had not looked closely at or worn before, I gasped; it was covered in umbrellas!

As I waited in line to buy treats with my son, something that used to make me feel so guilty, my son asked if we could also get a sticker, so I joined him in looking. My fingers closed over a sticker of . . . an umbrella! By now, I was really laughing.

I pressed it to my journal and we headed to the library, where a book sale was happening. A woman in a Christian tee-shirt smiled and winked and told me I could take anything I wanted for free.

The first book that caught my eye was one that had been in my Amazon cart forever, but I was afraid for my husband to see it-a popular book for women in abusive marriages.

He sees me, and He meets my needs! He is my only umbrella.

The Word of God Psalm 46: 1 "God is our refuge and strength, an ever present help in trouble."

The Comment from DC I love the picture of God as your only umbrella. Everyone else-every human-will let you down and disappoint you. But not God. Not ever.

God is your safe place. Your place of protection. God is your strength, providing His power whenever you need it. And He is always with you when you're in trouble. Always.

The Prayer to God Dear God, when it comes right down to it, I know You are the only One I can always rely upon. You are the only One who is always with me when I'm in trouble. Thank You for being my safe place, my refuge, and my ever present help in this trouble I'm going through.

The Truth from God God Has Work for You to Do

The Moment from God My worst moment. I was in sorry shape: weighing 70 pounds, double pneumonia, hypothermia 86 degrees, ketoacidosis. The hospital gave me a 10% chance of survival.

My husband left me on a ventilator in ICU and visited twice in 60 days. When I woke about day 60, I asked God why was I still on this planet? I was so done.

He replied, "you still have work to do, now rise up and walk." It's been hard but if God thinks I can, I'm darn sure I'll try.

The Word of God Jonah 2: 10, 3: 1-2 "And the Lord commanded the fish, and it vomited Jonah onto dry land. Then the word of the Lord came to Jonah a second time: 'Go to the great city of Nineveh and proclaim to it the message I give you.' "

The Comment from DC God saved Jonah, sinful and flawed Jonah, to use him. Jonah's job was to tell the wicked people of Nineveh about God's coming judgment so they would repent and follow God.

God did not put you on earth to suffer with the narc, a man who doesn't care if you live or die. In fact, the narc would prefer you die.

God put you on earth to serve Him. He has important work for you to do. God will save you from the narc so He can use you in His service.

The Prayer to God Dear God, it's hard to believe that You have work for me to do for Your Kingdom. Broken, traumatized, weak me? But I am willing to serve You. Once I get away from the narc-with Your help-I pledge to do what You want me to do for You.

DAY 51

The Truth from God God Will Use You to Help Other narc Victims

The Moment from God I've been married for 30 years and I took a leap of faith and separated from my abusive, pornified cheating "Christian" husband 5 years ago, with our youngest daughter who was 15 at the time.

I'm not sure if my husband is a diagnosable narcissist, but I know that he fits all the criteria(especially when he is in full blown acting out in his secret life of viewing pornography that I would always end up discovering).

All I ever wanted was to continue being close to my Lord and glorify Him with my life, in my vocation as a wife and mother. In the confusion of my marriage, my life was such a mess and I was such a mess, that it felt like it was impossible to be in the center of God's will and glorify the Lord.

I had become physically sick in my marriage, with migraines, and autoimmune illnesses, due to years of every form of abuse: physical, emotional, economic, sexual, psychological, spiritual. So much lying and gaslighting had my head spinning, some days I thought I was literally crazy.

I was so weary. I had an urgent sense that my one precious life was wasting away, and I wanted so desperately for my children to know me as a healthy vigorous woman and mom, like I had been prior to marriage.

After some encouragement and receiving a scholarship, I finally went to a conference/retreat for victims and started attending weekly support groups at my local shelter for abused women. I soon discovered that we all had so much in common.

During this time, I was asked if I wanted to volunteer and help with taking emergency calls from other victims, because they were short staffed. I could not believe that they thought I could actually help others while I was in the midst of hell myself! I felt like I should be in a better place before trying to help others!

Despite my insecurities, I agreed to volunteer and, 8 years later, I am still providing this service and helping women one-on-one! By helping others, I unknowingly helped myself, and the other women unknowingly helped me, and I was able to get to the healthy place where I could finally separate across the country from my abusive husband.

From the moment I left him, I started sleeping and eating better, feeling more alive, losing weight, and new practical resources and provisions opened up for me that I could've never imagined in my fear of leaving.

I have been blessed to receive extensive training as a domestic violence advocate over these years that has been personally therapeutic. I feel like I am living out the truth of Romans 8: 28.

The Word of God Romans 8: 28 "And we know that in all things God works for the good of those who love him, who have been called according to his purpose."

The Comment from God All the awful, indescribable pain and trauma you have suffered from the narc is not wasted. It has meaning and value in God's plan for you.

Once you leave and divorce the narc(and, like this lady, even before the divorce), God will use every bit of your experience to equip you to help other victims of abusive narcs.

All the hell you have endured will enable you to get others out of the hell they are still in.

The Prayer to God Dear God, it's encouraging to know that You will use my suffering to equip me to care for other victims of abusers. I will help others and they will help me!

The Truth from God If You Want to Get Well, Walk

The Moment from God When I was almost 20 years into my abusive marriage, I was studying John 5, which I had read many times before. When I read it this time, I suddenly felt a jolt from the Holy Spirit, unexpectedly telling me to leave my husband.

I am very cautious about taking Scripture out of context, or twisting it to say what I want it to say, but God's word is living and active, and I knew in my heart that he was speaking directly to me from that passage.

I was too afraid to leave at the time, but it changed my thinking about what God thought of my situation. He wanted me out of there. I never forgot it. Plus the abuse worsened, and I was able to leave my husband five years later.

The Word of God John 5: 6-8 "When Jesus saw him and knew he had been ill for a long time, he asked him, 'Would you like to get well?' 'I can't, sir,' the sick man said, 'for I have no one to put me into the pool when the water bubbles up. Someone else always gets there ahead of me.' Jesus told him, 'Stand up, pick up your mat, and walk!' "

The Comment from DC Jesus is asking you the same question he asked this lame man. "Would you like to get well? Would you like to leave the narc and be healthy and happy?"

It seems like a silly question. But it's not. I have talked to hundreds of abuse victims who have refused to leave their narcs. They don't want to get well. They don't want a life without their narcs.

I hope and pray you are not one of these women(and men)who choose to remain a victim forever. Jesus is asking you if you want to leave the narc. If you say yes and mean it, Jesus will get you out. He'll be with you every step of the escape journey.

The Prayer to God Dear God, I do want to leave the narc. I'm scared of leaving, scared to death. But I want to get out. I want a new life for me and my children. So, I am answering Jesus with: Yes!

ADDITIONAL RESOURCES

Other Books by David Clarke

20 Lies That Keep You With Your Abuser: Reclaiming Your Identity, Your Worth in Christ, and Your Freedom

Enough is Enough: A Step-by-Step Plan to Leave an Abusive Relationship with God's Help with William G. Clarke

Escaping Your Narcissist: What to Expect When You Divorce a narc

I Didn't Want a Divorce, Now What? How to Deal with Your Ex and Your Kids, Heal, and Get a Re-set with William G. Clarke

Stop Feeling Guilty For Your Divorce: Beat satan, Beat Shame, and Live in God's Grace and Freedom

My Spouse Wants Out: How to Get Angry, Fight Back, and Save Your Marriage with William G. Clarke

I Destroyed My Marriage: How to Win Your Spouse Back with William G. Clarke

Adult Children Who Break Your Heart: Bringing Your Prodigal Back to God and Back to You

Married But Lonely: Seven Steps You Can Take With or Without Your Spouse's Help with William G. Clarke

I Don't Want a Divorce: A 90-Day Guide to Saving Your Marriage with William G. Clarke

What to Do When Your Spouse says, "I Don't Love You Anymore": An Action Plan to Regain Confidence, Power, and Control with William G. Clarke

A Marriage After God's Own Heart

The Secret to Becoming Soulmates: A Couple's Devotional Journey to Spiritual Intimacy with William G. Clarke

Kiss Me Like You Mean It: Solomon's Crazy in Love How-To Manual with William G. Clarke

I'm Not Ok and Neither Are You: The 6 Steps to Emotional Freedom with William G. Clarke

Men Are Clams, Women Are Crowbars: The Dos and Don'ts of Getting Your Man to Open Up with William G. Clarke

Parenting is Hard and then you die: A Fun but Honest Look at Raising Kids of All Ages Right with William G. Clarke

Honey, We Need to Talk: Get Honest and Intimate in Ten Essential Areas with William G. Clarke

To order Dr. Clarke's books and video series, set up a phone advice session, and access his podcast and his YouTube Channel and other social media platforms, go to:

davideclarkephd.com

Or

davideclarkephd@gmail.com

For Dr. Clarke's complete, step by step escape from the narc plan, get these 3 books of his:

20 Lies
Enough is Enough
Escaping Your Narcissist

And to learn how to fight back against the narc's abuse, keep the narc from turning your kids against you, break the trauma bond, and get strong enough to leave the dirtball, get Dr. Clarke's online video series:
From Codependent to Independent
21 Things You Must Do Before Leaving Your narcissist(small n)